Profiles of the Presidents

ABRAHAM LINCOLN

★ ★ ★

Profiles of the Presidents

ABRAHAM LINCOLN

by Jean F. Blashfield

Content Adviser: Tim Townsend, Lincoln Home National Historic Site, Springfield, Illinois

Social Science Adviser: Professor Sherry L. Field, Department of Curriculum and Instruction, College of Education, The University of Texas at Austin

Reading Adviser: Dr. Linda D. Labbo, Department of Reading Education, College of Education, The University of Georgia

COMPASS POINT BOOKS ✦ MINNEAPOLIS, MINNESOTA

Compass Point Books
3722 West 50th Street, #115
Minneapolis, MN 55410

Visit Compass Point Books on the Internet at *www.compasspointbooks.com*
or e-mail your request to *custserv@compasspointbooks.com*

Editors: E. Russell Primm, Emily J. Dolbear, and Melissa McDaniel
Photo Researchers: Svetlana Zhurkina and Jo Miller
Photo Selector: Heidi Schoof
Designer: The Design Lab

Library of Congress Cataloging-in-Publication Data

Blashfield, Jean F.
   Abraham Lincoln / by Jean F. Blashfield.
      p. cm. — (Profiles of the presidents)
   Includes bibliographical references and index.
   ISBN 0-7565-0202-0 (hardcover)
      1. Lincoln, Abraham, 1809–1865—Juvenile literature. 2. Presidents—United States—Biography—Juvenile literature. [1. Lincoln, Abraham, 1809–1865. 2. Presidents.] I. Title. II. Series.
   E457.905 .B595 2002
   973.7'092—dc21   2001004734

Table of Contents

★   ★   ★

To Save the Nation

★　★　★

The task is done; the bound are free;
We bear thee to an honored grave,
Whose proudest monument shall be
The broken fetters of the slave.
— William Cullen Bryant

This poem was written in 1865 after Abraham Lincoln was murdered. A train carried the body of the sixteenth president of the United States to Illinois. Millions of people lined the train track. They saluted or prayed in silence as the big wheels rumbled past.

Lincoln had first been elected president five years earlier. He knew that his election would tear the young nation apart. He wanted to pull it together and keep it whole for all time.

When Lincoln became president, he did not plan

on freeing the 3 million black slaves in the South. But, over time, he decided that it was the only way to save the nation. So he broke their fetters, or chains, as mentioned in Bryant's poem.

▲ *The funeral train stopped in eleven cities on its thirteen-day journey from Washington, D.C., to Springfield, Illinois.*

This sculpture by ▶
Daniel Chester
French of a seated
Lincoln is in the
center of the
Lincoln Memorial in
Washington, D.C.

Lincoln's main task as president was the most challenging any U.S. president has faced. He had to make certain that there was still a United States for future presidents to govern.

The Early Years

★ ★ ★

Abraham Lincoln was born on February 12, 1809, in a log cabin near Hodgenville, Kentucky. His father was Thomas Lincoln, the son of an early settler in the area. His mother was Nancy Hanks. He had an older sister named Sarah. His brother, Thomas, was born in 1812 and, sadly, died that same year.

As a young child, Abraham (he never liked the nickname Abe) played in the woods. He also learned how much hard work it took to run a farm in

▲ *Thomas Lincoln, Abraham's father*

A replica of the Knob Creek, Kentucky, cabin where Lincoln lived from 1811 until 1816.

the wilderness. As soon as he was old enough, he began to help as much as he could. He planted seeds and pulled weeds.

When Abraham was six, he started school. He and Sarah walked several miles to the nearest school. There they learned the basics of reading and writing. But after a few months, the Lincoln children had to leave school. They were moving to Indiana where their father thought it might be easier to earn a living.

It was 1816, and Abraham was seven when the Lincolns headed north to Indiana. Along the way, the boat carrying their furniture sank in the Ohio River. The only belongings that made it to Indiana were what two horses could carry.

They spent their first winter in Indiana in a shack

made of branches, grass, and mud. It was open on one side, where a fire was kept burning night and day. During that bitter winter, Abraham helped his father clear the land. Big and strong for his age, he became good at using an ax to cut down trees. The Lincolns used the logs to build a one-room cabin.

But life continued to be hard for the family. A disease

▲ The Lincoln family moved their belongings by boat down the Ohio River, much like the settlers in this illustration.

Young Abraham Lincoln worked very hard to help his mother and father. One of his chores was cutting wood.

soon swept through the region. Abraham's mother died. Abraham would later say, "All that I am or hope ever to be, I owe to my angel Mother."

But Abraham had no time to stop and feel sad. He and his father still had to get the farm up and running. He also often worked for other farmers, helping to clear their fields. Meanwhile, Sarah tried to take over her mother's work indoors.

It soon became clear to Thomas Lincoln that he needed a wife and that his children needed a mother. He went back to Kentucky where he married a woman named Sarah Bush Johnston.

Sarah Johnston's first husband had died, and she already had three children of her own. But from the day she arrived in Indiana and hugged ten-year-old Abraham and twelve-year-old Sarah, she was their new mother. She could not read or write, but she made sure that Abraham and Sarah went to school as often as they could.

▲ *Sarah Bush Johnston Lincoln, the stepmother of Abraham Lincoln*

That wasn't very often. During his whole life, Abraham Lincoln spent less than one year in school, but his stepmother made sure that books were around.

Abraham enjoyed reading. From his earliest childhood,

This oil painting, ▶ titled Boyhood of Lincoln, *shows a young Abraham Lincoln reading by firelight.*

he had loved words. When he heard a new word, he would try to figure out what it meant. He would move it around in his mouth as if it were a piece of candy. Then he would use it whenever he could.

As a teenager, Abraham grew tall and thin. By the end of his teens, he was nearly 6 feet 4 inches (193 centimeters) tall yet he weighed just 180 pounds (82 kilograms). But he had powerful muscles from the many years he had spent cutting down trees.

In 1828, Abraham's sister Sarah died in childbirth. She was the second important person in his young life who had died. He found it difficult to shake off his sadness. In later years, he would lose two of his own children. Each time, he sank into a fog of hopelessness.

▲ The Rail Splitter *by famous painter Jean Leon Gerome Ferris*

Lincoln on the ▸
Ohio River flatboat

Later that year, Abraham helped take a boat loaded with cargo to New Orleans, Louisiana. Abraham and his friend Allen Gentry moved the heavy boat with long oars.

It took brute strength. They sailed down the Ohio River to the Mississippi River, and down the Mississippi into the Deep South.

New Orleans was the first big city Abraham had ever seen. It was there that he saw human beings sold as slaves. It was a sight he would never forget.

▲ *A slave auction, where slaves were bought and sold like livestock.*

Stepping into Politics

★ ★ ★

When Abraham was twenty-one, his family moved west to Illinois. Thomas was drawn by the idea of living on the open prairie. He thought it would be easier to make a living there. Abraham wasn't sure what he wanted, but he did not think it was farming.

Lincoln made another boat trip to New Orleans with a man who owned a store in the town of New Salem, Illinois. When he returned, he moved to New Salem. Lincoln began working in a store and lived in a room in the back.

In New Salem, Lincoln became friends with Mentor

Abraham Lincoln continued his self-education by reading everything he could get his hands on.

◄ *A reconstructed nineteenth-century farm at Lincoln's New Salem Historic Site, in Petersburg, Illinois*

Graham, the local schoolteacher. Graham helped him find good books to read. Then the two men would talk about them. Whenever Lincoln wasn't working, he was reading.

He also joined the New Salem Debating Society. The members would choose a subject to talk about in a formal way. Then each person would present an argument in favor of one side or another. During these **debates,** Lincoln became a confident speaker. He also learned to think on his feet.

One of the subjects he and his friends debated was slavery. More and more people in the North were becoming angry that slavery was allowed in the South. The people who firmly believed that slavery should be outlawed were speaking up. Lincoln had to admit that it wasn't a subject he thought about much. It just wasn't part of his world.

Within eight months of moving to New Salem, Lincoln decided to see if his talents might be well suited to politics. He decided to run for a seat in the state **legislature.**

Lincoln traveled around the district speaking to any gathering of people. He told everyone that he was a humble man, just like them.

Black Hawk, chief ▲
of the Sauk Indians

But soon the state of Illinois put out a call for troops. They needed help to force some Sauk Indians to move from Illinois into Iowa. Lincoln signed up and stopped running for political office to join the military.

The other men in Lincoln's unit saw him as a natural leader and soon elected him captain. He served for three months but saw no real action. He returned home just two weeks before the election.

Most of the people of New Salem had voted for him, but the district included many other towns as well. So

★

Lincoln came in eighth out of the sixteen men running.

    After this disappointment, Lincoln and a man named William Berry bought their own store. Sadly, after a few months, the store failed, and then Berry died. Lincoln was left to pay off the store's debts by himself. It took him fifteen years, but he paid off every penny. This was probably one reason he became known as "Honest Abe."

    In 1834, Lincoln ran for the state legislature again. At that time, each district elected several people. He was one

▲ *The Berry–Lincoln store at Lincoln's New Salem State Historic Site* of four men who won. So he set off for Vandalia, then the capital of Illinois.

One of the most important issues being talked about in Vandalia was **abolition,** or ending slavery. At that time, people from southern Illinois controlled the legislature. Most of them agreed with the South about slavery. But Lincoln was certain that slavery was wrong.

Being in the state legislature was not a full-time job, so Lincoln decided to become a lawyer. Few lawyers actually went to law school at that time. Instead they were trained by a skilled lawyer. It took Lincoln two years to learn enough to take the tests to be a lawyer. He received his law license in 1836 and started taking on cases.

When the Illinois capital moved to Springfield in 1837, Lincoln moved as well. It was in Springfield that Lincoln met Mary Ann Todd of Lexington, Kentucky. Both Mary and Abraham were very interested in politics.

▲ *William Lloyd Garrison headed the American Anti-Slavery Society, and was publisher of* The Liberator, *a paper calling for the abolition of slavery.*

Abraham Lincoln as a lawyer in court

This portrait of Abraham and Mary Todd Lincoln was painted shortly after they moved into the White House in 1861.

Unlike Lincoln's family, the Todds were well-to-do. Some of Mary's relatives did not think she should marry someone from such a poor background. Despite these protests, Mary and Abraham were married on November 4, 1842.

This painting of Lincoln as a traveling lawyer is titled Pilgrims of the Law.

Lincoln became a successful lawyer in Springfield. People liked his ability to be both serious and relaxed in court. Soon, he left the state legislature and became a traveling lawyer instead. He would study a case and then argue it in court, all within a few days. He felt like an actor who had to write his own lines.

As a traveling lawyer, Lincoln got to know the voters—and the voters got to know him. This was helpful when he ran for the U.S. House of Representatives in 1846. Lincoln ran as a member of the Whig Party and beat the Democratic challenger by more than 1,500 votes. He was delighted to be going to Washington, D.C. He thought perhaps that was where his future lay.

Mary and their two sons, Robert and Edward, went with him. Unfortunately, the capital city was a very crowded place. The four of them had to move into a

★

single room. After only three months, Mary left with their sons to live with relatives in Kentucky.

▲ *The first battle of the Mexican War was fought at Palo Alto, Texas, on May 8, 1846.*

In Congress, Lincoln made a name for himself by speaking against the Mexican War. The United States had gone to war against Mexico in 1846. Most Americans supported the war, but Lincoln did not think that the war was right. He did not believe that Mexican soldiers had ever actually invaded the United States. Lincoln was right, but Congress wasn't interested in what he said because the United States got a lot of new land after winning the war.

Lincoln did not run for a second term in Congress. Instead, he returned to Illinois and practiced law. He became one of the most successful lawyers in Illinois.

In one important case, he was hired to defend a railroad company. The railroad had built the first bridge across the Mississippi River, but a steamboat had crashed into the bridge. The steamboat company sued the railroad, saying that the bridge was a danger to its boats. Lincoln argued that the nation must be free to expand westward. This would not happen if the river could not be bridged. He won the case, helping to open the West to settlement.

Abraham Lincoln ▶ won an important case in court and helped open the way for western expansion.

The Slavery Debates

★ ★ ★

Lincoln once called slavery a "monstrous injustice." But he was not a strict **abolitionist**. He wanted to sit down with slave owners and reason with them. He thought slavery should be banned in any new states that entered the Union, but he did not think Congress had the power to end slavery in states where it already existed.

Stephen A. Douglas, a U.S. senator from Illinois, introduced a bill in Congress that became known as the Kansas-Nebraska Act. Kansas and Nebraska were both ready to

▲ *Stephen Douglas*

become states. Douglas's bill would allow the people of each state to choose for themselves whether to allow slavery.

Suddenly, Lincoln had found a purpose in his career. He would work to stop the spread of slavery in the West.

Abolitionists who were against the Kansas-Nebraska Act were among those who formed a new political party,

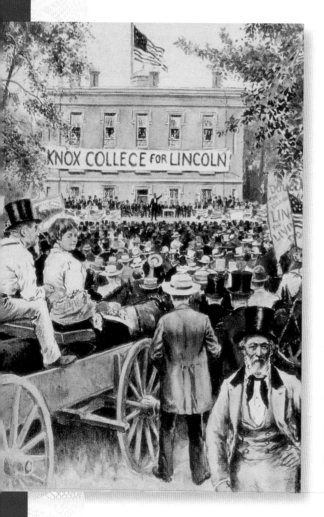

A Lincoln-Douglas debate was held at Knox College in Galesburg, Illinois, on October 7, 1858.

called the Republican Party. Lincoln joined the Republicans and decided to run against Stephen A. Douglas in the 1858 U.S. Senate race. In one of his most famous speeches, he talked about the need to end slavery. "'A house divided against itself cannot stand,'" he said, quoting the Bible. "I believe this government cannot endure, permanently half slave and half free."

Lincoln challenged Douglas to a series of seven debates. Both men were excellent speakers who argued their case well. As many as 15,000 people watched each

debate in person. The rest of the state and the nation read about them in the newspapers.

During the debates, Douglas argued that people had the right to decide the slavery issue for themselves. Lincoln said that slavery itself was a "moral, a social, and a political wrong." He thought it was the duty of the government to stop slavery from spreading into new states.

The election in November 1858 was very close. Lincoln won by just 14,000 votes. But at the time, it was not the people who chose U.S. senators. It was the state

▲ A slave overseer supervises slaves picking cotton. Lincoln believed that no person had the right to own another human being.

legislature. The Democrats controlled the legislature, and they gave the election to the Democrat—Stephen Douglas.

Lincoln was disappointed at having lost again. But people all over the country had heard about the Lincoln-Douglas debates. Lincoln was no longer a little-known politician from Illinois. Now he was famous.

The 1860 presidential election was coming up. The Republicans chose Lincoln to run.

The Democratic Party was split between Northerners and Southerners. Stephen A. Douglas was the candidate of

Election poster for Lincoln–Hamlin campaign of 1860 ▼

the Northern Democratic Party and John C. Breckinridge was the candidate of the Southern Democratic Party. John Bell ran for president as a member of the Constitutional Union Party. None of the men could get enough support to beat the man from Illinois. Lincoln promised Southerners that he would not outlaw slavery in the South.

The Southerners did not believe Lincoln. They threatened to **secede**, or withdraw, from the Union if Lincoln won. The Northerners did not think they would actually do it.

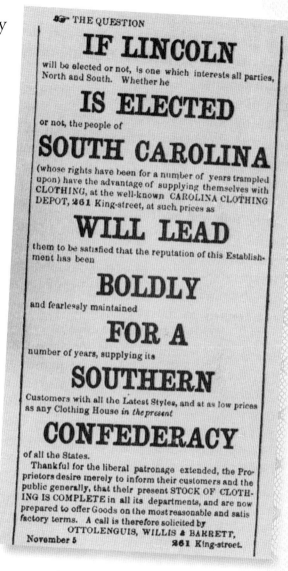

The Carolina Clothing Depot of Charleston used this creative method to advertise against the election of Abraham Lincoln.

The election was held on November 6, 1860. Soon after midnight, it became clear that Lincoln would be the next president. Hannibal Hamlin would be vice president. Lincoln had not won a single southern state.

United States, 1861
- States
- Territories

President Jefferson Davis and other leaders of the Confederacy

The southern states had been serious about leaving the Union if Lincoln won. On December 20, South Carolina became the first state to secede. Before Abraham and Mary Lincoln left Springfield for Washington on February 11, 1861, six

◀ *Abraham Lincoln was sworn in as the sixteenth president of the United States on March 4, 1861.*

more states had followed South Carolina's example. They joined together to form the Confederate States of America. In time, eleven states would join this separate nation.

When Lincoln took the oath of office in March 1861, he still believed that the southern states would come back into the Union. In his **inaugural,** or swearing-in, speech, Lincoln promised that he would not do away with slavery where it was legal. But he also said that the United States was a permanent nation. He said that the southern states had no right to secede.

The Civil War

★ ★ ★

On April 12, 1861, just before dawn, Southern troops fired on the Union's Fort Sumter, in the harbor of Charleston, South Carolina. The day that Lincoln had hoped would never arrive had come. The nation was split. The two parts—the Union and the **Confederacy**—were at war with each other.

Fort Sumter, ▶
South Carolina,
was the scene of
the opening battle
of the American
Civil War.

Children watch Union cavalrymen water their horses in the stream at Bull Run, the scene of two battles during the Civil War.

Little happened in the first few weeks of the war. Both the North and the South were busy getting their armies together. On July 16, Lincoln ordered an attack on **Confederate** troops in northern Virginia, near Bull Run Creek. Neither side was ready, but the Southern soldiers were more experienced. The Union troops had to turn around and go back to Washington.

Lincoln himself had little military experience. He put General George B. McClellan in charge of the eastern part of the Union army after the defeat at Bull Run (also known as Manassas). McClellan was a big-city man who

President Lincoln ▶
met with General
McClellan at
headquarters on
the battlefield of
Antietam in 1862.

thought he knew more than Lincoln. He built a strong
army, but he did not like sending his men into battle.
Lincoln began to read books about how to win battles.
He hoped that he could understand how to fight the war.

During this time, Lincoln's home life was also difficult. His two younger sons came down with a deadly
disease called typhoid fever. Tad got better, but Willie
became weaker and weaker. When Willie died, Mary was

so sad she hardly got out of bed. Lincoln was sad, too, but he still had to focus on the war.

The war was also being fought farther west. Union troops were not letting Confederate boats go up the Mississippi River. Lincoln knew that the West was important to the future of the country. He was set on keeping it out of the hands of the Confederacy.

For many years, the northern states had wanted to open the West to settlement. But the southern states had been afraid that this would create new antislavery states. If that happened, the slave-owning states would eventually be outnumbered in Congress.

With Lincoln's support, Congress passed the

Homestead Act in 1862. It gave settlers the right to claim 160 acres (65 hectares) of federal land in the Midwest and Great Plains. Any person who claimed land had to live on it for five years. Then he or she owned it, free and clear. Thousands of people moved west to claim land.

Congress urged Lincoln to outlaw slavery. But he refused. He thought that would be against the **Constitution.** Some Union generals tried to outlaw slavery in the areas they controlled. But Lincoln thought such bold moves would keep the Union from ever being mended. If he freed the slaves, border states between the North and the South would probably secede, too.

Over time, however, Lincoln realized that the only

way to save the nation was to get rid of slavery. More than anything else, slavery was what had caused the southern states to secede.

In July 1862, Lincoln told his advisers that he was thinking of freeing the slaves by presidential **proclamation.** Most agreed that it was a good idea. But they thought he should wait until after the North won a big battle.

On September 17, Confederate general Robert E. Lee's troops faced General McClellan's Union troops in Maryland. It was a battle that the North called Antietam and the South called Sharpsburg. Thousands of men were lost in what became the single bloodiest day of the Civil War.

◀ *A group of slaves outside a cabin*

★

▲ The Battle of
Antietam

Lincoln used the battle as an excuse for two major decisions. McClellan had not followed Lee as Lee had headed back into Virginia after the battle, so Lincoln decided to replace him. More importantly, Lincoln decided to call the battle a victory for the North.

On September 22, 1862, the president stated he would free the slaves in any Confederate state that did not return to the Union by January 1, 1863.

Weeks and months passed, but no Confederate

◄ *Abraham Lincoln's Emancipation Proclamation was the first step toward outlawing slavery in the United States.*

state asked to rejoin the Union. On New Year's Day, Lincoln signed the **Emancipation** Proclamation. This freed the slaves in the Confederacy. It went into effect at midnight that night.

But it did not free all slaves. Those in border states were not covered by the proclamation. They were not freed until three years later, when the Thirteenth **Amendment** to the Constitution outlawed slavery throughout the nation.

Though the slaves in the Confederacy were now officially free, the war was not over. Confederate troops had started moving into the North in June 1862.

By the summer of 1863, they had reached southern Pennsylvania. At the little town of Gettysburg, they ran into Union troops. For three bloody days, Northern and Southern troops fought at Gettysburg. By the time the battle ended on July 3, more than 51,000 men had been wounded or killed. Gettysburg was the farthest north Confederate troops reached during the war.

Later that year, a new national cemetery was established at Gettysburg. On November 19, Lincoln gave a speech at the opening of that cemetery. Lincoln's speech was less than three minutes long, but his Gettysburg Address is considered one of the most moving speeches ever delivered. He made it clear that he believed a new, better nation could be born out of the war. "This nation, under God, shall have a new birth of freedom," he said.

But before that nation could be born, the war still

had to be won. In March 1864, Lincoln put General
Ulysses S. Grant in charge of the entire Union army.
By this time, Lincoln had realized that the South wasn't
going to just give up and return quietly to the Union.
The slave-owning states would have to be defeated to end
the war. He gave that task to Grant.

▲ *The Battle of Gettysburg*

Abraham Lincoln ▶
delivering the
Gettysburg
Address, painted
by Jean Leon
Gerome Ferris

In November 1864, General Grant lost 54,000 men while trying to advance just 6 miles (10 km) in Virginia. The public became angry at Lincoln. He feared he might not be reelected. He was afraid that if he lost the election, slaves might lose their chance for freedom.

Then, just before the election, Union general William T. Sherman captured Atlanta, Georgia. The backbone of the South was broken, and Lincoln was reelected. He would be free to carry out his ideas.

On March 4, 1865, Lincoln was sworn in as president for the second time. In his inaugural speech, he tried

▲ *General Ulysses S. Grant*

Confederate general Robert E. Lee and Union general Ulysses S. Grant met in the parlor of Wilmer McLean's house in Appomattox, Virginia, to fix the terms of surrender.

to explain how the war should end. He did not think the South should be punished for having stuck to its beliefs. There should be no revenge. "With **malice** toward none; with **charity** for all," he said, "let us strive on to finish the work we are in; to bind up the nation's wounds."

On April 9, the Civil War ended when Confederate general Robert E. Lee **surrendered** to General Grant. Four million people who had been slaves were suddenly free. Some people could not stand that idea.

On April 14, Abraham and Mary Lincoln went to see a play at Ford's Theatre in Washington. They were seated

The presidential box at Ford's Theatre in Washington, D.C.

John Wilkes Booth ▲ in a box, an area closed off from the regular seats. As they watched the play, a man named John Wilkes Booth crept into the box and fired at the back of Lincoln's head.

Booth leaped from the box onto the stage and ran out. He fled into Virginia, where he was killed several days later.

Lincoln was carried to a house across the street. There he died early the next morning.

For the People

★ ★ ★

Had Lincoln lived, he might have been able to convince the North to be gentle with the defeated South. But his murder put an end to that hope. It would be years before the southern states were brought fully back into the Union, and decades before the anger eased.

◄ This portrait of Abraham Lincoln by George P.A. Healy hangs in the State Dining Room at the White House.

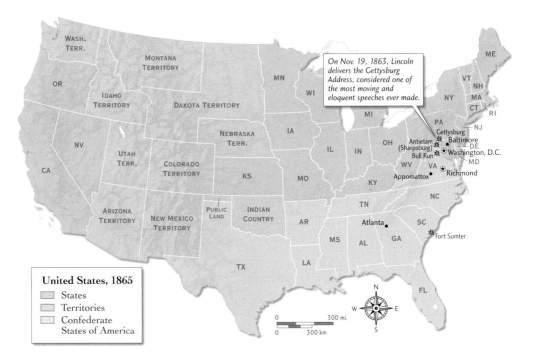

On Nov. 19, 1863, Lincoln delivers the Gettysburg Address, considered one of the most moving and eloquent speeches ever made.

United States, 1865
- States
- Territories
- Confederate States of America

President Abraham Lincoln believed that holding the United States together was important for the whole world. He thought other countries needed to see that **democracy** can work even when one part of the nation disagrees with another part.

Lincoln had made this point in the Gettysburg Address. He ended that speech by saying that the dead buried there had given their lives "that government of the people, by the people, for the people, shall not **perish** from the earth."

GLOSSARY

★ ★ ★

abolition—banning slavery

abolitionist—someone who supported the banning of slavery

amendment—change

charity—kindness

Confederacy—the Southern states that fought against the Northern states in the Civil War

Confederate—a supporter of the Confederacy

Constitution—the document stating the basic laws of the United States

debates—formal arguments

democracy—government in which the people elect the leaders

emancipation—freedom

inaugural—swearing in

legislature—the part of government that makes or changes laws

malice—desire to cause pain or distress

perish—to become ruined or destroyed

proclamation—an official announcement

secede–withdraw from

surrendered—gave up

ABRAHAM LINCOLN'S LIFE AT A GLANCE

★ ★ ★

PERSONAL

Nickname: Honest Abe and Illinois Rail-Splitter

Born: February 12, 1809

Birthplace: Hodgenville, Kentucky

Father's name: Thomas Lincoln

Mother's name: Nancy Hanks Lincoln

Education: Less than one year of formal education in his lifetime

Wife's name: Mary Todd Lincoln

Married: November 4, 1842

Children: Robert Todd Lincoln (1843–1926); Edward Baker Lincoln (1846–1850); William Wallace Lincoln (1850–1862); Thomas "Tad" Lincoln (1853–1871)

Died: April 15, 1865

Buried: May 4, 1865, at Oak Ridge Cemetery, Springfield, Illinois; his remains were moved to the permanent tomb/memorial in the same cemetery in 1871

PUBLIC

Occupation before presidency:	General store clerk and lawyer
Occupation after presidency:	None
Military service:	Joined the army and served three months during the Black Hawk War in 1832
Other government positions:	Member of Illinois general assembly, representative of Illinois in the U.S. House of Representatives
Political party:	Republican
Vice Presidents:	Hannibal Hamlin (1861–1865), Andrew Johnson (1865)
Dates in office:	March 4, 1861–April 15, 1865
Presidential opponents:	Senator Stephen A. Douglas (Northern Democrat), Vice President John C. Breckinridge (Southern Democrat), former U.S. senator John Bell (Constitutional Union Party), 1860; General George B. McClellan, 1864
Number of votes (Electoral College):	1,865,908 out of 4,685,030 (180 of 303), 1860; 2,218,388 out of 4,031,195 (212 of 233), 1864
Writings:	Emancipation Proclamation, Gettysburg Address

★

Abraham Lincoln's Cabinet

Secretary of state:
William H. Seward
(1861–1865)

Secretary of the treasury:
Salmon P. Chase (1861–1864)
William P. Fessenden (1864)
Hugh McCulloch (1865)

Secretary of war:
Simon Cameron (1861–1862)
Edwin M. Stanton (1862–1865)

Attorney general:
Edward Bates (1861–1864)
James Speed (1864–1865)

Postmaster general:
Montgomery Blair (1861–1864)
William Dennison (1864–1865)

Secretary of the navy:
Gideon Welles (1861–1865)

Secretary of the interior:
Caleb B. Smith (1861–1863)
John P. Usher (1863–1865)

ABRAHAM LINCOLN'S LIFE AND TIMES

★ ★ ★

LINCOLN'S LIFE

February 12, **1809**
Lincoln is born in a
one-room log cabin in
Hodgenville, Kentucky

Moves with his family **1816**
across the Ohio River
(above) to Indiana

Nancy Hanks **1818**
Lincoln dies

WORLD EVENTS

1809 American poet and
short-story writer
Edgar Allen Poe is
born in Boston

1810

1810 Chile fights for its
independence from
Spain

1812– The United States
1814 and Britain fight
the War of 1812

1814– European states
1815 meet in Vienna to
redraw national
borders after the
Napoleonic Wars

LINCOLN'S LIFE

Father marries Sarah   1819
Bush Johnston (below)

WORLD EVENTS

1820

1820   Susan B.
Anthony
(right),
a leader of
the American
woman
suffrage
movement,
is born

1821   Central
American
countries gain
independence
from Spain

1824   Mexico becomes
a republic

1826   The world's first
photograph is taken
by French physicist
Joseph Niépce

Sister, Sarah, dies in   1828
childbirth; makes his
first trip to New
Orleans

1827   Modern-day
matches are
invented by
coating the end
of a wooden stick
with phosphorus

1830

The Lincoln family   1831
moves to Illinois and
settles near Decatur

1829   The first practical
sewing machine
(right) is invented
by French tailor
Barthélemy
Thimonnier

LINCOLN'S LIFE			WORLD EVENTS
Moves to New Salem, Illinois, and works as a store clerk	1830	**1830**	
			1833 Great Britain abolishes slavery
Is elected to the Illinois general assembly as a member of the Whig Party	1834–1842		
Becomes a lawyer	1836		1836 Texans defeat Mexican troops at San Jacinto (above) after a deadly battle at the Alamo
Moves to Springfield and begins law practice (left), with John Todd Stuart	1837		1837 American banker J. P. Morgan is born
Is admitted to practice law in U.S. Circuit Court	1839	**1840**	1840 Auguste Rodin, famous sculptor of *The Thinker* (below), is born
Begins new law partnership with Stephen T. Logan	1841		
Seeks Whig nomination for U.S. Congress but is unsuccessful	1843		

LINCOLN'S LIFE

WORLD EVENTS

Dissolves his law
partnership with
Logan and starts his
own practice — 1844

Is elected to the U.S.
House of Represen-
tatives as a member of
the Whig Party — 1846

Returns to Springfield
to practice law in
partnership with
William H. Herndon — 1848

1848 — *The Communist
Manifesto,* by German
writer Karl Marx
(above), is widely
distributed

Is elected to Illinois
legislature — 1849

1850

1852 — American Harriet
Beecher Stowe (above)
publishes *Uncle
Tom's Cabin*

LINCOLN'S LIFE

WORLD EVENTS

Works to organize the
Republican Party in
Illinois — 1854

Runs for
U.S. Senate but
loses to Stephen A.
Douglas (above) — 1858

1858 — English scientist
Charles Darwin
(above) presents his
theory of evolution

Presidential Election Results:	Popular Votes	Electoral Votes
Abraham Lincoln	1,865,908	180
John C. Breckinridge	848,019	72
John Bell	590,901	39
Stephen A. Douglas	1,380,202	12

November 4, elected
sixteenth president of
the United States — 1860

1860

1860 — Austrian composer
Gustav Mahler is born
in Kalischt (now in
Austria)

December 20, South
Carolina becomes the
first state to secede
from the Union

LINCOLN'S LIFE

1861 — March 4, is sworn in as president

April 12, the Civil War begins when Fort Sumter is fired upon

1863 — January 1, issues the Emancipation Proclamation

November 19, gives the Gettysburg Address on the battlefield (right) in Gettysburg, Pennsylvania

1864 — November 8, is reelected president

1865 — March 4, delivers his Second Inaugural Address

April 9, the South surrenders, ending the Civil War

April 14, is shot while attending a play at Ford's Theatre (right)

April 15, dies shortly after 7 A.M.

WORLD EVENTS

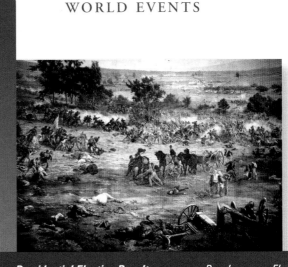

Presidential Election Results:	Popular Votes	Electoral Votes
Abraham Lincoln	2,218,388	212
George B. McClellan	1,812,807	21

1865 — Lewis Carrol writes *Alice's Adventures in Wonderland*

UNDERSTANDING ABRAHAM LINCOLN AND HIS PRESIDENCY

★ ★ ★

IN THE LIBRARY

Heinrichs, Ann. *The Emancipation Proclamation.*
Minneapolis: Compass Point Books, 2002.

Holzer, Harold, editor. *Abraham Lincoln the Writer: A Treasury of His Greatest Speeches and Letters.* Honesdale, Penn.: Boyds Mills Press, 2000.

Murphy, Jim. *The Long Road to Gettysburg.*
New York: Clarion Books, 2000.

Sullivan, George. *Picturing Lincoln: Famous Photographs that Popularized the President.* New York: Clarion Books, 2000.

ON THE WEB

The History Place Presents Abraham Lincoln
http://www.historyplace.com/lincoln/index.html
For a wide variety of pictures relating to Lincoln and his life

Abraham Lincoln Quotes
http://home.att.net/~rjnorton/Lincoln78.html
For a selection of statements from the president

The Lincoln Museum Online
http://www.thelincolnmuseum.org/index2.html
For the life and legacy of Abraham Lincoln

News of Abraham Lincoln's Death
http://starship.python.net/crew/manus/Presidents/al/alobit.html
For official dispatches from *The New York Times*
regarding Lincoln's death

Lincoln Home National Historic Site
http://www.nps.gov/liho/
For information on the Lincolns and their home as well as
a travel guide for those planning to visit the historic site

LINCOLN HISTORIC SITES
ACROSS THE COUNTRY

**Abraham Lincoln Birthplace
National Historic Site**
2995 Lincoln Farm Road
Hodgenville, KY 42748
270/358-3137
To see a log cabin like the one
in which Lincoln was born

**Ford's Theatre National
Historic Site**
900 Ohio Drive, S.W.
Washington, DC 20024-2000
202/426-6924
To see the historic theater
where Lincoln was shot

Gettysburg National Cemetery
97 Taneytown Road
Gettysburg, PA 17325-2804
717/334-1124
To see memorials to the dead
and the spot where Lincoln
made his most famous speech

**Lincoln Home
National Historic Site**
413 South Eighth Street
Springfield, IL 62701-1905
217/492-4241 ext. 221
To see artifacts from Lincoln's
life in the only house he ever
owned

Lincoln Memorial
900 Ohio Drive, S.W.
Washington, DC 20024
202/426-6841
To see the giant statue
honoring Lincoln

THE U.S. PRESIDENTS
(Years in Office)

★ ★ ★

1. George Washington
    (March 4, 1789–March 3, 1797)
2. John Adams
    (March 4, 1797–March 3, 1801)
3. Thomas Jefferson
    (March 4, 1801–March 3, 1809)
4. James Madison
    (March 4, 1809–March 3, 1817)
5. James Monroe
    (March 4, 1817–March 3, 1825)
6. John Quincy Adams
    (March 4, 1825–March 3, 1829)
7. Andrew Jackson
    (March 4, 1829–March 3, 1837)
8. Martin Van Buren
    (March 4, 1837–March 3, 1841)
9. William Henry Harrison
    (March 6, 1841–April 4, 1841)
10. John Tyler
    (April 6, 1841–March 3, 1845)
11. James K. Polk
    (March 4, 1845–March 3, 1849)
12. Zachary Taylor
    (March 5, 1849–July 9, 1850)
13. Millard Fillmore
    (July 10, 1850–March 3, 1853)
14. Franklin Pierce
    (March 4, 1853–March 3, 1857)
15. James Buchanan
    (March 4, 1857–March 3, 1861)
16. Abraham Lincoln
    (March 4, 1861–April 15, 1865)
17. Andrew Johnson
    (April 15, 1865–March 3, 1869)

18. Ulysses S. Grant
    (March 4, 1869–March 3, 1877)
19. Rutherford B. Hayes
    (March 4, 1877–March 3, 1881)
20. James Garfield
    (March 4, 1881–Sept 19, 1881)
21. Chester Arthur
    (Sept 20, 1881–March 3, 1885)
22. Grover Cleveland
    (March 4, 1885–March 3, 1889)
23. Benjamin Harrison
    (March 4, 1889–March 3, 1893)
24. Grover Cleveland
    (March 4, 1893–March 3, 1897)
25. William McKinley
    (March 4, 1897–
    September 14, 1901)
26. Theodore Roosevelt
    (September 14, 1901–
    March 3, 1909)
27. William Howard Taft
    (March 4, 1909–March 3, 1913)
28. Woodrow Wilson
    (March 4, 1913–March 3, 1921)
29. Warren G. Harding
    (March 4, 1921–August 2, 1923)
30. Calvin Coolidge
    (August 3, 1923–March 3, 1929)
31. Herbert Hoover
    (March 4, 1929–March 3, 1933)
32. Franklin D. Roosevelt
    (March 4, 1933–April 12, 1945)

33. Harry S. Truman
    (April 12, 1945–
    January 20, 1953)
34. Dwight D. Eisenhower
    (January 20, 1953–
    January 20, 1961)
35. John F. Kennedy
    (January 20, 1961–
    November 22, 1963)
36. Lyndon B. Johnson
    (November 22, 1963–
    January 20, 1969)
37. Richard M. Nixon
    (January 20, 1969–
    August 9, 1974)
38. Gerald R. Ford
    (August 9, 1974–
    January 20, 1977)
39. James Earl Carter
    (January 20, 1977–
    January 20, 1981)
40. Ronald Reagan
    (January 20, 1981–
    January 20, 1989)
41. George H. W. Bush
    (January 20, 1989–
    January 20, 1993)
42. William Jefferson Clinton
    (January 20, 1993–
    January 20, 2001)
43. George W. Bush
    (January 20, 2001–)

INDEX

★ ★ ★

ABOUT THE AUTHOR

Jean F. Blashfield has worked for publishers in Chicago, Illinois, and Washington, D.C. A graduate of the University of Michigan, she has written more than ninety books, most of them for young people. Jean F. Blashfield has two college-age children and lives in Delavan, Wisconsin.